MANAGING PRACTICE

Report on the Management of Practice Expertise Project

Patricia Kearney
with a Preface by Denise Platt CBE,
Chief Inspector of Social Services Inspectorate

Contributors: Gwen Rosen and Gerry Smale,
NISW

National Institute for Social Work

Managing Practice
Report on the Management of Practice Expertise Project

Published 1999
by the National Institute for Social Work
5 Tavistock Place, London WC1H 9SN
www.nisw.org.uk
email info@nisw.org.uk

© National Institute for Social Work

All rights reserved. No part of this publication may be reproduced or transmitted in any form or by any means, electronic, mechanical, photocopying, recording or otherwise, or stored in any retrieval system of any nature, without prior permission of the publisher.

ISBN 1 899942 34 3

Cover designed by Pat Kahn

Printed by Meridian Print Centre Ltd, Derby

Preface

Front-line managers are the keystones of any social services organisation. Their quality and competence makes a significant difference to its performance. They manage the primary tasks and activities of the organisation. They have a key role in determining whether standards of practice are consistently maintained. They support staff engaged in complex, personally demanding practice, and ensure that staff are continually developed in knowledge based practice. They need to take a balanced approach to their work. Without this they can add to the separation that can occur within an organisation and the poor or non-existent collaboration with others. There are important issues to be considered for their training and development.

In this Department of Health funded project, the National Institute for Social Work has completed some important work looking at managing and developing social work practice. This book describes some crucial management development areas for front-line managers, which arise from this work.

I believe strongly that this neglected area must have the attention it deserves, because service quality depends on it. We in the Department of Health will be considering what action we need to take to support the findings of this work and I urge you to do so, in order to motivate, assist and support staff to develop competence and skill in the most challenging of professional tasks.

Denise Platt CBE
Chief Inspector of the Social Services Inspectorate
October 1999

Acknowledgements

Thanks to all the staff who worked with us in the Consortium agencies. This account has depended on their enthusiasm, generosity and, above all, their professional expertise.

Patricia Kearney, Gwen Rosen and Gerry Smale
National Institute for Social Work
October 1999

Contents

Introduction	1
Main Findings	2
The Context of Change	5
The Background to the Project	7
The Management of Practice Expertise Project	10
Management Issues Arising During the Project	18
Discussion	22
Key First-line Manager Development Areas	29
References	32

Introduction

This account considers how practice is managed within the personal social services. It sets out the findings of the National Institute for Social Work's Management of Practice Expertise Project, and the central role for first-line managers in developing and sustaining practice standards. The background described includes details of some of NISW's development work over the last decade. It also sets out the key areas for first-line manager development that took shape during the Project.

Main Findings

Good and poor practice often exist within the same organisation, suggesting that senior management responsibility for overall standards of practice is only one of a number of significant variables.

- The work carried out in the Project suggests that the competence of the first-line manager and staff is a key variable. It is possible to find poor practice in a good team, although this is usually held in check in some way. But it is very difficult for a good practitioner to sustain good practice in a poor team with poor team management.

- The application of general management theory to the effective running of organisations assumes that someone somewhere in the organisation knows how the job should be done. We conclude that within each team somebody has to have expert knowledge to lead staff and act as a good practice model. Whether this person is called a manager, team leader, or senior practitioner is not crucial. But it is essential that this person is involved in the professional and management decisions that have to be made about the best use of all resources in order to respond to social problems at the local level. That is, achieving the tasks of the organisation.

- Managing changes in the organisation is often at the expense of practice management. We repeatedly experienced examples of the way that re-re-organisation overtook the plans of staff and drew the attention of managers from direct practice and its management.

Although designed to solve service delivery problems, the way such changes were managed often led to them being self defeating.

- Ambiguity often exists over the degree of autonomy that can or should be exercised by different units within organisations.

- There is an urgent need for the development of knowledge about and appropriate management responses to persistent poor performance and 'failing units' within organisations.

- The implications of this work are not confined to social services departments. Whatever form social work and social services take in the future it will involve teamwork amongst direct practice staff, and with citizens and staff in other organisations. These teams and their practice will need to be led and managed.

- The skill mix in teams needs to be constantly reviewed. The presence of good local administrative and financial management personnel lets social work staff, care staff and their managers focus on the content and quality of the services they deliver. Sometimes administrative staff were working well beyond their job descriptions to operate as office managers, to great effect.

- Vertical slice work (bringing together managers and staff from the different levels in the organisation) can be a powerful way of clarifying expectations, exploding myths about different people's beliefs, accelerating the flow of information and solving problems blocking the development of practice and service delivery.

- The team plays a crucial role in effective practice. The key difference between good and poor practice appears to rest with the first-line manager and the team's abilities.

Specifically this means their shared understanding of the task and their capacity to work on it. It does not depend on procedural direction handed down through the wider organisation. The wider organisation will nurture this shared understanding by vision and collective leadership.

- First-line managers are the 'keystone' of the organisation. They manage the primary tasks and work on the margins of the different parts and activities of the organisation. From this key position their job is to hold together what can often seem like different worlds. If they take the side of one at the expense of maintaining a working relationship with another, they contribute to destructive segmentalisation within the organisation and poor or non-existent collaboration with others.

The Project developed a number of themes which are discussed more fully in a set of issues papers which look at :

- The Functions of Front-line Managers
- The Team
- The Role of Senior Managers and the Wider Organisation
- Issues of Integrity.

These are published separately as a companion document to this report, *Integrity, the Organisation and the First-Line Manager*.

The Context of Change

The statutory social services find themselves facing difficult questions: is a care manager the same as a social worker? What is the role of the qualified social worker within a statutory agency nowadays? What is the role of managers in these agencies and what do they need to know? Previous assumptions about the nature of professional expertise and the organisational context within which it operates need re-evaluation and re-definition. Managers have a responsibility for staff development and work force planning, as well as ensuring that the organisation is informed by and about the direct work it undertakes. These can only be achieved with trust and a shared language and purpose between managers and first-line staff.

The last decade has seen considerable changes in the role of local government. New legislation regarding the welfare of children, care in the community and fundamental policy shifts on the future of welfare have had an enormous impact on the statutory social services. Traditional assumptions about the nature of their work, the skills and expertise required, and about their relationship with other care agencies and corporate colleagues have been challenged.

These changes have demanded the acquisition of new skills or the adaptation of old ones and have required scrutiny of the conceptual and ethical frameworks that underpin the work of social care agencies. As with all change, there has been accompanying anxiety that there may be no place for already established expertise and knowledge.

The Project developed from a growing awareness that although attention was being paid to general management development in the personal social services, improvements were not necessarily experienced by first-line staff. This suggested that the impact of management development might be improving the internal running of organisations but not having a significant impact on the quality of practice and service delivery. The Project wanted to find out the nature of the relationship between management and practice in the social services. How robust is it and how can it be best sustained?

Moreover, the recurring picture of practice from NISW's research and development work, Social Service Inspectorate Reports and Joint Reviews has been that the quality of practice continues to be inconsistent across social service departments and organisations. Poor and indifferent practice can be found in the same departments as good practice.

The Background to the Project

These issues were exemplified in NISW's evaluation of the social services' response to the Hillsborough Disaster (Newburn 1993) and subsequent development work. There was agreement among the participants in this development work that there was no proper recognition in their organisations of the need to develop practice expertise. Much practice and staff development can and does take place in the workplace but often despite, rather than fostered by, management action. Participants in the evaluation project concluded that the development of 'practice expertise' had become a 'closet activity'. For example, advanced practice training was often undertaken at the worker's expense with little support and even overt hostility from managers. Such training was nearly always undertaken on an individual basis, the transfer of learning to other colleagues being left to chance. There were few common standards for development and training. First-line workers also felt unsupported, feeling that their managers were not credible professional consultants.

These findings focused attention on the role of managers and their development, and specifically on two key inter-related questions:

- Should the functions of line management, professional consultation and personal support be separated?

- What kinds of approaches to management enable staff to develop and sustain their practice expertise?

We asked these questions through:

- a survey of the supervision arrangements and policies in social service departments (Kearney 1996a)
- a more detailed study of practice sites engaged in 'expert practice' (Kearney 1996b)
- a consensus development conference and exchange workshops. These brought managers, practitioners and management developers together to look at the relationship between the different aspects of management, supervision and practice development (NISW/LGMB 1995).

This work is detailed elsewhere. In brief, however, it indicated the relative scarcity of management training opportunities within the personal social services. Where this was available, it was usually at a general management level and often offered corporately across the local authority. Managers said they wanted this and more. They wanted help with how they might best manage and sustain the practice they were responsible for. They wanted management development which specifically addressed the welfare environment. That is, where complexity, distress and irreconcilable differences are always present (Darvill 1997).

The survey indicated that few social services departments had formal arrangements integrated within their management structures and policy frameworks to ensure the support and development of practice, or to ensure that 'expert' practice informed the strategies and policies of the department as a whole. Some thought that experienced staff did not, or should not, require formal supervision. Others were aware that once they explored the quality of supervision they were inextricably involved in a whole range of activities. These included:

- the effectiveness and appropriateness of the service provided
- the function and use of management information
- practice-led service development
- the contribution of social services to the corporate group
- the support and development of managers and their supervision.

In many departments supervision was so taken for granted that, paradoxically, it was not explicitly integrated within the organisation, for example through appraisal or service review, and was not monitored or evaluated.

The survey found that most available management development programmes, based externally or developed in-house, offered technical competency around organisational maintenance or at best 'managing people'. Conference participants considered that management in the statutory social services has unique characteristics, requiring particular management skills. These include the capacity to integrate technical skills within the professional context of social work and social care. Conference participants considered that this capacity for integration is necessary for a critical approach to management theory and the confidence to adapt and develop management of practice models.

Furthermore, there seemed to be little opportunity for managers to keep abreast of professional information or of integrating this within their management of practice.

The Management of Practice Expertise Project

This work helped to shape the three year Management and Development of Practice Expertise Project (1995-1998) supported by the Department of Health and a consortium of three social service departments. Department 'A' was in a large county council, Department 'B' an industrial, metropolitan authority, and Department 'C' an inner city authority. We cannot claim that they are representative of all departments, but we did work with people in very varied circumstances and still found many common features of the relationship between management and practice.

Aims of the Project

- To develop management dedicated to developing and sustaining expert social work practice and social services delivery.
- To work with managers and practitioners to develop their practice in implementing recent changes in policy and legislation.

The Consortium Organisations

The three authorities provided resources for the training and development work that would be undertaken with them during the Project. They also gave us access to staff at all levels to reflect on the management issues raised through the development of practice, specifically to identify 'what promotes and what inhibits the development of good practice'.

The three departments all identified their first-line managers in fieldwork services as the primary targets for practice development for the Project. Depending on the organisation's structure, first-line managers went under a variety of job titles and positions. The departments' focus echoed our experience of the important role played by first-line managers. The first stage of the Project did not directly involve day-care or residential teams, and only one multi-organisation team. However, we think that many of the issues that emerged are common to first-line managers across all social care settings. This was our experience in the second stage of the Project which included day care and multi-organisation and multi-disciplinary team managers. (We have subsequently applied the Project's findings in work with managers across all settings and found many themes to be common to all.)

The Project Timetable

We were aware that the major and ongoing changes within social service departments must be affecting front-line practice and its management. We needed to see the 'current state of play'. That is, what were managers managing on a daily basis? We asked each Consortium agency to identify two teams where practice was considered to be sound and who were interested in working with us. We undertook to provide the training and development needs the teams would identify in their work with us (stage 1).

The front-line managers of these teams formed a group that worked with us to identify and develop the skills they considered necessary for their work (stage 2) which we then used as a basis for a first-line management development programme offered across the department (stage 3).

Throughout this timetable, senior managers in the department were involved in a variety of ways. Debriefing meetings with directors and senior managers were held throughout the Project to review this development work and to discuss emerging issues. Organisation development work also included 'vertical slice' meetings bringing together practitioners, first-line managers, their immediate senior managers and members of the directorate management team, to work on specific issues and problems related to the development of practice. These took place during phases two and three of the Project. The senior managers from the three organisations met as one group with project staff twice during the Project. They looked specifically at the practice examples from the Project and considered the themes and issues emerging.

Finally, senior managers and the other participating groups worked with us at the end of the Project to disseminate its findings within their departments and to agree the final report to the Department of Health. Drafts were discussed with participant managers and staff and their responses incorporated in the issues papers *Integrity, the Organisation and the First-Line Manager*.

Poor Practice

We agreed a procedure in the event of coming across practice that caused us concern. This was, that we would draw the attention of those involved to our concern and our reasons for this. If the matter was not righted at this stage, we would involve the next tier of management, and so on, up to directorate level. Staff involved would always be informed of our concern and the action we planned to take.

Stage 1

The teams we worked with varied in size and service responsibility depending on their Department's structure. They were:

Department A

an area-based Children and Families service
an area-based Community Care team

serving different areas

Department B

the department-wide Juvenile Justice team
an area-based Community Care team

Department C

an area-based Children and Families service
an area-based Community Care service

serving the same geographical area and based on the same site

---

Development work with these teams included on-site observations of their work and discussion with them to identify their development needs. We organised and provided training and development workshops as identified. During this process we mapped their areas of work with them and discussed how they used their resources, the major issues confronting them and what they saw as the opportunities and difficulties affecting their work.

Workshop topics varied: some involved presentation of new information and knowledge by outside professionals, for example on the new Mental Health Act Code of Practice. Some gave staff the opportunity to discuss work with service user organisations. Some were forums set up with seniors and peers across the organisation and partner organisations to look at how they might best work together. In this instance, the Project provided time and resources for teams to strengthen their own professional networks. Teams said that this was an activity they did not usually have the time, energy or other resources to undertake. However, multi-disciplinary and multi-organisation teams had more opportunity to undertake networking as part of their usual routine than colleagues in the mainstream of the organisation.

Stage 2

We held a residential workshop with all the first-line managers whose teams had participated at stage 1. Common issues emerging from the Project were reviewed and we drew up an initial draft of a development agenda for first-line managers. This formed the basis of some key management development areas. These were subsequently tested in the development programmes carried out in two of the departments.

Stage 3

In Departments A and B we provided development programmes for first-line managers. Each was of ten days duration, undertaken over ten months.

Department A

Participation in this stage was offered to all first-line managers as one of five options in the department's management development strategy. The NISW programme content was based on the development agenda drawn up at stage 2 of the Project and was agreed with senior managers and development staff. Timing, content and style of delivery was negotiated with the participants. Twelve of the department's 16 first-line managers chose to work with the NISW programme.

Content: The first-line managers agreed that they wanted to consider:

- the management of change
- setting boundaries for the team
- the team's autonomy within the organisation
- managing the 'difficult' team member.

Delivery: Some of this work was undertaken by the whole group, which was an opportunity for managers at this level across the department to work together. Whilst managers met within their operational divisions, this was usually for 'business' meetings, not their professional development or to look at how they managed the work of their teams. Although managers did not usually meet outside their service delivery boundaries, they found much to share when they met together in the Project.

Managers also had the choice of working with us outside of this group. We met managers on their own, with their own line manager and with their teams in whole or in part (for example, with the senior practitioners in the team). We held skills sessions, practice discussions, consultations and live observation of the work that first-line managers undertook with their teams.

Department B

All first-line managers, 31 in total, attended the programme.

Content: The curriculum was planned with the participating managers and three particular areas for development were agreed with them. These were:

- group supervision
- managing change and innovation
- re-focusing children and families services.

Delivery: The entire group met to plan the development agenda and continued to meet together throughout the programme. Participants also opted for one of three groups:

- group supervision: an experiential 'skills based' sequence
- managing change and innovation: a sequence to consider and apply the literature and theory of managing change
- re-focusing children and families services: a task based group that contributed to the department's development work on this topic.

Participants were also able to choose some individual work, which included direct observation of their team management and consultation on development work and on poor performance issues.

Department C

A similar programme to the above was agreed by senior managers and planned. However their agency was unable to sustain the programme despite a number of attempts to get it started. Instead, a series of individual consultation sessions were carried out with managers, the terms of which were negotiated at the beginning of the consultation process.

The training materials developed and used with teams in this stage of the Project are published separately as a companion document, *Managing Team Development: a short guide for teams and team managers*.

Management Issues Arising During the Project

Inevitably there were delays and difficulties that affected the smooth running of the Project and its timetable. However, these provided insights into the 'management of practice' and the management of organisations. They also highlighted an urgent need for the development of knowledge about, and appropriate management responses to, persistent poor performance and 'failing units' within the organisation. They are discussed below.

Managing changes in the organisation at the expense of practice management: The problems we experienced in developing a first-line manager training programme in Department C were a symptom of the many problems they were experiencing. The department was going through a series of rapid changes. Indeed it was in a constant state of flux, although as far as we could tell, the patterns of first-line practice stayed much the same. It was also subject to external inquiries and reviews, which have since reported and led to further major changes being undertaken, both within the department and in the authority as a whole. An analysis and discussion of the complex issues involved in this department are beyond the scope of this report. However, we should observe that in this department, and elsewhere, we repeatedly experienced examples of the way that re-re-organisation overtook the plans of staff and drew the attention of managers away from practice and its management. Although designed to solve first-line problems, the way such strategies were managed often led to them being self-defeating.

Ambiguous autonomy: In two of the three departments we experienced some difficulty in gaining entry to teams identified by senior managers as participating sites. In both departments area teams were, in effect, able to veto our involvement with them. Stalling or delaying participation achieved this in one team, either deliberately or unintentionally. In another, similar behaviour concluded with a more overt decision to withhold co-operation. In either situation senior management could have forced the issue but they, and we, doubted whether this would have led to effective collaboration. These relatively early experiences drew attention to the ambiguity that exists over the degree of autonomy exercised by different units within these organisations.

Management expectations: Whilst not claiming that we saw a complete spread of management styles, we nevertheless did experience some significant differences of approach. We have drawn some conclusions from these observations, for example where senior managers gave unambiguous messages about what they expected, staff were more likely to comply.

Vertical slice work: This refers to the way we worked with the departments to tackle some key issues and debrief about the development of practice activities. For example, we invited first-line managers to identify ways the organisation's practices could be changed for the better. We then brought them together with their managers and members of the directorate group to review these issues. This can be a powerful way of clarifying expectations and exploding myths about different people's beliefs. It accelerates the flow of information and solves problems blocking the development of practice and service delivery.

First-line staff were frequently surprised that senior managers had actually heard and acted upon what they were saying. Staff found it difficult, and sometimes impossible, to be frank with senior managers who generally overestimated the degree to which staff felt comfortable with them. Our observations have suggested a number of contributory factors to this unease, not least the difficulties of operating within large, complex bureaucracies. However, professional confidence was often at a low ebb within teams, with uncertainty about professional autonomy as a major contributor.

Poor performance and 'failing units': We came across examples of practice that caused us serious concern. These included:

- poor standards of direct practice
- practitioners and first-line managers prevented from undertaking what they considered to be best practice by departmental procedures
- instances of unsatisfactory working across operational and service divisions that first-line staff had not been able to improve.

Some of these examples were observed by us and others were raised with us by the staff we worked with. In accordance with the protocol, we referred these to the next management level, or beyond. In one situation this was tackled swiftly and directly when it reached directorate level. In another the response was protracted, and complicated. This response highlights the dangers of redesigning the system rather than confronting issues of poor performance directly. We also saw how difficult this is when management authority is diffuse and complicated by wider organisational and political considerations.

Discussion

General Management Theory

The application of general management theory to the effective running of organisations assumes that someone somewhere in the organisation knows how the job should be done. In industry technical experts such as design and production engineers, marketing departments and cost accountants guide the general manager. In the Health Service, 'Performance Management' is being developed within a context where clinical practitioners, the health professionals, understand how the job should be done. In social services and social work organisations we need to ask who knows how the job should be done. Or to put the question another way: who if not first-line managers know how staff should carry out the work?

Managers have to assume that field social workers, typically the staff with the highest professional qualification, are only trained to HND level, equivalent to the first two years of an undergraduate degree. This level of training does not compare well to a graduate profession such as teaching, or postgraduate qualified occupations such as medical practitioners. Managers cannot assume that their staff have a level of education, training and expertise that equips them for fully independent professional practice, although clearly some practitioners reach such a level of sophistication.

The level and extent of social work training is not our concern here, but within each team somebody has to know how the job should be done and act as a leader and role model for staff. Whether this person is called a team leader, a manager or senior practitioner is not crucial. But it is essential that this person is involved in the professional and management decisions that have to be made about the best allocation of resources to respond to social problems at the local level: the achievement of the tasks of the organisation.

Skills Mix in Teams

This needs to be constantly reviewed. This clearly applies to staff working directly with the public and their managers, but other so called 'support staff' also need explicit consideration. First-line management and staff can be greatly supported by able administrator staff. In the Project, first-line managers and their teams were better able to focus on the content and quality of the services they delivered where they had the benefit of good administrative and financial management support. Sometimes administrators were working well beyond their job descriptions to operate as office managers, to great effect. Early in the Project some senior managers recognised that the introduction of the 1990 National Health Service and Community Care and 1989 Children Acts, and internal restructuring had placed more and more organisational maintenance, administrative tasks and financial responsibilities on first-line managers. Despite this it was often tacitly assumed that they would carry on supervising staff as before, when in practice this had become increasing impracticable.

These problems were sometimes compounded where administrative staffing was a casualty of financial constraints. Under these circumstances, managers and staff whose experience and training qualify them to be engaged in direct practice and service delivery have often become reluctant administrators, weakening all aspects of the organisation's functioning. The introduction of supervision policies were in part a response to these dilemmas.

Supervision and Leadership of Teams

This issue has been a constant thread running throughout our work. For some it is synonymous with the management of practice, but it is also clear that practice is influenced, for better or for worse, by other dimensions of management practice. The Project demonstrated that effective supervision and team management involves:

- organisation of time and team participation
- effective facilitation of team meetings
- team leadership.

We recognise the need to move beyond the limited view of supervision as either confidential one to one sessions concentrating on the supervisee's personal development, or conversely a session devoted to checking procedural compliance.

The management of effective practice requires the mobilisation and application of the team's resources as well as attention to individual practice. It also requires the manager to know what staff are doing and how they are doing it. This involves attention to the content of practice, that is the methods and processes the worker engages in. Workers need a finely tuned sense of professional anxiety to be able to reflect on their feelings and use them in understanding their work in the relationships they form with service users and significant others. Discussion of this with an informed third party is more than a check on effective performance. It is an essential dimension of effective practice itself.

We observed some managers paying attention to seemingly small and maybe simple tasks. They usually described this attention to us as 'obvious', with all the potential for being undervalued that the description implies. We saw it as expertise hard won.

These team managers created *effective and dynamic environments* for their teams by:

- attending meetings on time
- expecting all staff to:
  - attend on time
  - attend unless they give appropriate reasons
  - to come prepared with necessary documents for the meeting
  - preparing all staff for the agenda.

Managers *facilitated* team meetings by ensuring:

- clear communication throughout the meeting
- differences are openly discussed; staff are confident that their views are being listened to; the manager is able to clarify and enlarge workers' contributions
- boundaries are adhered to, that is professional discussion and a focus on direct work of the team members is protected from being overtaken by organisational business or by conversations about wide generalities
- an environment where there is trust between team members and agreement to carry out their different tasks.

They led the group by *demonstrating*:

- the confidence to make decisions in a meeting and demonstrate clearly why these decisions have been made

- an expectation of agreeing and undertaking action
- clarity about what are team tasks and the limits and purpose of the team
- respect for other people's skills, experience and specialist knowledge within the team.

These are management skills of a high order. Acquiring them can be hindered in a number of ways: there is an unspoken (sometimes spoken) rule that 'you're not a social worker now'. Very few first-line managers receive help in developing these qualities and the necessary sense of authority and autonomy they depend on. We found a minority of managers in the programme with group or family work training who had transferred those skills from their direct practice. New managers may not always be confident that their practice skills provide legitimate experience and knowledge to support their new role.

Professional Knowledge and Collective Wisdom

The Project echoed the findings in our earlier work, that staff often found professional knowledge was hard to come by. These sources ranged from published research, including practice discourse, to the ready availability of expertise within their own agencies. There were several elements to this.

- Time to gather, consider, analyse and apply such material was hard to come by. There were few formal opportunities, such as research or practice forums, within the agencies. Workers in specialist or multi-organisation settings were most likely to have such opportunities, including cross-organisation forums, and access to specialist publications. We found that when managers were provided with access to material and the opportunity to reflect on it, they were keen to do so.

- Managers were often unsure if they should be interested in professional knowledge as they were 'no longer social workers'. However, as leaders of individual and team practice, managers wanted access to up-to-date professional knowledge. During the time of the Project, a number of initiatives got under way: for example, NISW's on-line information service; Research into Practice; Research Matters. We noted that individuals with Internet access made enthusiastic use of these initiatives. However, this was usually in their own time and on home equipment.

- Teams and first-line managers involved in the Project began to hold practice focused meetings, where research and casework were presented. For most of the first-line managers, the Project offered them a rare opportunity to consider themselves as a peer group that could share collective wisdom and experience.

Managing Poor Performance

A number of first-line managers wanted help with managing 'difficult' staff members. Meeting with other first-line managers specifically to discuss their collective task, share skills and offer encouragement to each other, proved particularly helpful in this area.

We noted that many first-line managers felt isolated when dealing with persistent poor performance. This was so even when the first-line manager's own manager was actively involved and supportive. We met with several such pairs of managers about this issue.

It did seem that first-line managers were expected, either overtly or unintentionally, to contain persistent poor performance because the department otherwise faced protracted action that the local authority and elected members might be reluctant to take forward. This had the effect, particularly where departments had few lines of communication between front-line and senior staff, of making persistent poor performance an issue of the first-line manager's own competence. In this situation, they often felt that they were poor professional supervisors or that they needed better management skills or 'more training'. Acknowledgement of the difficulties facing the department as a whole, human resources development frameworks and links with human resources development staff would have supported first-line managers more effectively.

First-line managers are required to tread a careful tightrope between facilitating a group and line managing a team. No other level of management faces quite this duality of role between the requirements of the organisation, including elected members, and those of front-line staff and service users. This is one of the significant ways in which first-line managers are (or fail to be) the keystone of the organisation in the bridge between policy makers and the public.

Key First-line Manager Development Areas

We summarise below the main areas of skill and knowledge identified through our observations and confirmed through discussions with first-line managers and their managers. It is not intended to be an exhaustive list of first-line manager competencies. It focuses on areas that managers need to develop, maintain and be supported in, in order to develop and sustain good practice in social work and social services delivery.

- *Clarifying the task:* expanding and maintaining knowledge of methods of practice and service delivery includes:
  - how the job is being done by others
  - evidence supporting different approaches to practice
  - feedback from all service users, clients and other key players.

- *Use of management information on workload and deployment of resources*, for example:
  - referrals: numbers – sources – patterns
  - nature and incidence of local social problems
  - staff resources
  - devolved budgets
  - other team resources
  - identification of local resources
  - other organisations and voluntary organisations.

- *Supervision skills and strategies*, including:
  - professional consultation

- monitoring performance
- staff support.

- *Managing change and innovation*, including:
  - change agent skills and knowledge
  - service development
  - practice innovation
  - surviving re-re-reorganisation.

- *Managing collaboration and partnerships*, including:
  - work with other organisations, commissioning/contracting services
  - team working, dovetailing services and interventions with others
  - work with service user groups, constantly reviewing the task and way that it is performed.

- *Developing courage and integrity*, through:
  - giving usable feedback to staff on their actions and behaviour to improve their performance
  - seeking and receiving feedback from staff, collaborating organisations, and service users to improve the effectiveness of the team and the first-line manager's own management performance
  - acting in counter-intuitive ways when working with people. This refers to the need for managers and practitioners to engage with rather than avoid problems involving confusion, anxiety and personal pain. This is crucial for sustaining the effectiveness of staff who are expected to work with people who have complex problems; who are in major crisis and suffering loss or deprivation and at a time when they are experiencing, or trying to produce major changes in their lives. This also involves being particularly good at dealing with the day to day problems involved in the normal stresses and strains of being part of the organisation.

If managers cannot be seen to confront the problems staff experience in their work and in their organisations, why should they expect their staff to be able to confront the typically more complex and demanding problems of service users and their social circumstances?

References

Darvill G ed (1997) **Managing Contradiction and Avoidance: discussion paper and self audit.** ADSS/NISW

Kearney P (1996a) **The Management of Practice Expertise: project report.** NISW

Kearney P (1996b) **Managing Expert Practice: a study of four practice sites.** NISW

Newburn T (1993) **Making a Difference? social work after Hillsborough.** NISW

NISW /LGMB (1995) **The Great Divide: managing practice or managing the department?** Conference Papers. NISW

Rosen G ed (1999a) **Managing Team Development: a short guide for teams and team managers.** NISW

Rosen G ed (1999b) **Integrity, the Organisation and the First-Line Manager.** NISW